ECOGRAPHICS

OVER POPULATION

Izzi Howell

W
FRANKLIN WATTS
LONDON • SYDNEY

Franklin Watts

First published in Great Britain in 2019 by The Watts Publishing Group

Copyright © The Watts Publishing Group 2019

Produced for Franklin Watts by
White-Thomson Publishing Ltd
www.wtpub.co.uk
01273 479982

Editor: Izzi Howell
Designer: Clare Nicholas
Cover designer: Steve Mead

Getty: leungchopan 8, Atlantide Phototravel 12, Mordolff 13, JeremyRichards 19, peeterv 24, naveen0301 27;
Shutterstock: Fabian Plock 5, Nord Photo 7t, Habrus Liudmila 7b, John Wollwerth 11, Jazzmany 15, thomas Koch 17,
Wildeside 20, Hari Mahidhar 23, TonyV3112 29.

All design elements from Shutterstock.

Every attempt has been made to clear copyright. Should there be any inadvertent omission
please apply to the publisher for rectification.

ISBN 978 1 4451 6642 1

Printed in Dubai

Franklin Watts
An imprint of
Hachette Children's Group
Part of The Watts Publishing Group
Carmelite House
50 Victoria Embankment
London EC4Y 0DZ

An Hachette UK Company
www.hachette.co.uk
www.franklinwatts.co.uk

Contents

What is overpopulation?.................. 4

Population density........................ 6

(FOCUS ON) Singapore 8

Births and deaths 10

(FOCUS ON) Niger 12

(FOCUS ON) Russia 13

Migration 14

(FOCUS ON) Syria 16

Resources 18

(FOCUS ON) Drought-resistant crops.............. 20

Water 22

Cities 24

(FOCUS ON) Mumbai 26

Solutions 28

Glossary 30

Further reading and websites 31

Index 32

What is overpopulation?

The current world population is around 7.6 billion and increasing every day. Some people are starting to worry if the Earth will be able to support such a huge population in the future. We may be reaching a stage of overpopulation, in which the amount of resources needed to support a population is more than a location can provide.

Resources

People need natural resources to survive. These resources include water, fuel, building supplies and fertile land for growing food (see pages 20–21). We also need space to live. As the world population grows, it puts pressure on the supply of these resources.

Population growth

For a long time, the world's population increased slowly. In the 1800s, the population shot up and has continued to grow very quickly ever since. At the moment, it is growing by 1 billion people every 15 years. If population growth continues at this rate, there will be around 9.7 billion people on Earth by 2050.

Improvements in healthcare and sanitation in the nineteenth century lowered death rates dramatically, which resulted in a huge population increase.

Population in millions

10,000
8,000
6,000
4,000
2,000
0

500 BCE 0 1000 1500 1800 1900 1950 1975 1999 2025

Year

Reasons for overpopulation

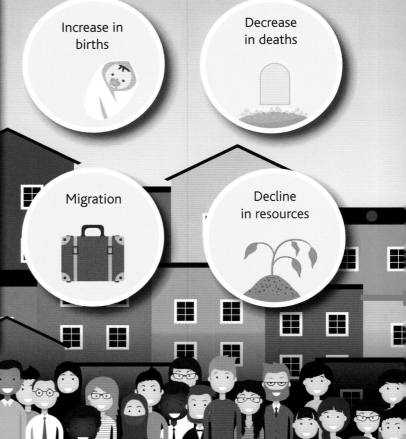

Increase in births

Decrease in deaths

Migration

Decline in resources

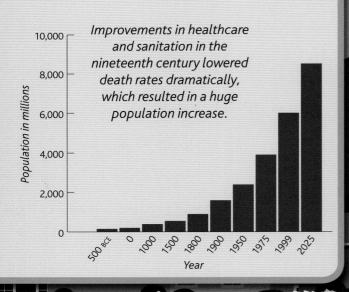

Around the world

Overpopulation affects certain areas more than others because the world population is not evenly distributed. More people live in less economically developed countries than in more economically developed countries. Natural resources are not evenly distributed either. Less economically developed countries can't always afford to purchase the resources that their citizens need. Small amounts of resources are shared by a large number of people in these countries, meaning that some people do not get enough.

These children live in Angola – the country with the second highest rate of population growth. Angola is experiencing problems with poverty and lack of access to clean drinking water and sanitation.

Consequences of overpopulation

| Destruction of natural resources | Climate change | Pollution | Human suffering |

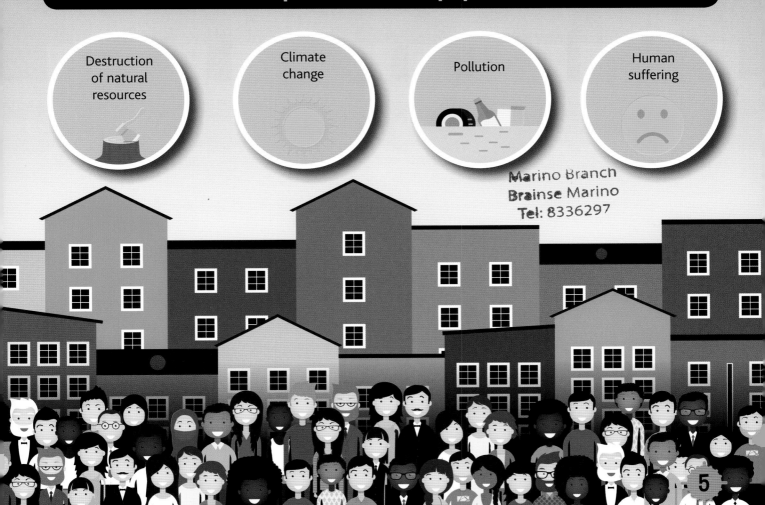

Marino Branch
Brainse Marino
Tel: 8336297

5

Population density

Population density is the average number of people living in a square kilometre of land. Less and more economically developed countries can both have high population densities.

Economy

Some areas have high population densities for economic reasons. They may be rich in resources or there may be many jobs that attract people to the area. For example, many people have moved to Hong Kong for work, making the population density rise to 6,700 people per square km. Its high density is also due to its small size (see page 7).

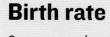

Birth rate

Some areas have high population densities because of high birth rates (see page 10). For example, there are 1,100 people per square km in Bangladesh. This is because of high birth rates in the 1960s and 1970s.

Hard-to-live-in areas

Places with extreme climates, such as deserts and polar regions, have low population densities as few people live there. This is also true of areas that are hard to build in, such as high, rocky mountains.

Greenland has the lowest population density in the world, with just 0.03 people per square km. The hostile, icy weather and lack of jobs mean that few people live there.

Large countries

Geographical size affects population density. Large countries, such as Australia, appear to have low population densities, as their population is spread out over a big area. However, if we look at individual parts of these countries, there may be areas of high density in cities and very low density in rural regions.

Australia

Population – nearly **25 million**
Size – **3 million** square km
Average population density –
3 people per square km
Population density in the city of Sydney –
1,070 people per square km

The area of Monaco is limited by the sea on one side and mountains on the other.

Small countries

Very small countries, such as Monaco, have very high densities as their population is focused into an area of only a few square km. However, a few small countries, including Monaco and Gibraltar, are also tax havens (areas with very low rates of tax). This attracts people to register as residents even when they don't live there. This makes the country's population density seem higher than it really is.

FOCUS ON Singapore

Singapore is an island country in Southeast Asia. It has the third highest population density in the world, due to its geography and economy.

FACT FILE

SIZE:
719.9 square km

POPULATION:
5,898,000

POPULATION DENSITY:
8,192 per square km

Geography

The country of Singapore is made up of Singapore Island and around sixty small islands. Most of the land is found on Singapore Island, which is also home to the city of Singapore. Its size is limited by the space available on the islands.

Singapore Island

Singapore (city)

Settlements

The largest settlement in Singapore is the city of Singapore. There are many other smaller towns built across the islands. Most people in Singapore live in urban areas. Housing in these areas is mainly made up of high-rise flats, which are an efficient way of fitting many homes into a small area of land.

New high-rise flats are built in Singapore to replace old, less space-efficient housing.

80%
of the population of Singapore live in high-rise flats.

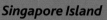

Economy

Singapore has a very strong economy. Many people come from all over the world to work in its finance, shipping and construction industries. Students are also attracted to Singapore to study in its many schools and universities.

More people

Singapore has a low birth rate, but a high migration rate (see pages 14–15). This helps to keep the population stable. Without immigration bringing new people into the country, Singapore's population would fall, as more people die there every year than are born.

13 out of every 1,000 people in Singapore are immigrants.

Resources

The small size of Singapore affects its supply of natural resources. It has little room for farming, so around 90 per cent of food is imported. Singapore also has almost no lakes or rivers. Its fresh water supply comes from rainwater or is imported from Malaysia. Singapore is starting to remove the salt from sea water and reuse more waste water to increase its water supply.

Pollution

If everyone in Singapore drove cars, the traffic and pollution would be terrible. Instead, the government has invested in public transport systems to encourage people to leave their cars at home. Drivers who choose to use their cars are heavily taxed and pay tolls on certain busy roads.

Many trains in Singapore are built on raised tracks to save space on the ground.

Births and deaths

World and country populations change over time because of births and deaths. High birth rates and low death rates make the population increase. High death rates and low birth rates make the population fall.

Lack of education about family planning

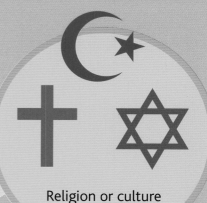

Religion or culture

Births

Less economically developed countries often have high birth rates for several reasons.

High infant and child death rates (people have more children in case some die in childhood)

In Somalia, each woman has an average of nearly 6 children. However, nearly 1 in 10 infants dies before its first birthday.

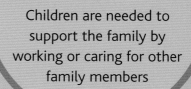

Children are needed to support the family by working or caring for other family members

Deaths

The death rate is the number of deaths per year. People die for many reasons, including old age and disease. People are also killed in wars and by natural disasters, such as earthquakes. Lack of access to clean water or enough food can also be fatal.

Growth

In some areas, the population is growing because of high birth rates. This is often the case in less economically developed countries. Around the world, populations are also increasing because fewer people are dying. This is because life expectancy has improved due to advances in medicine (see right) and improvements in living conditions.

Medicine

Today, people are living longer because of new treatments for diseases and conditions that may have killed them in the past. Vaccinations in childhood prevent people from catching potentially fatal diseases such as tuberculosis and measles. Medicine and operations treat serious conditions such as cancer and heart disease. Better conditions mean that fewer women and babies die in childbirth.

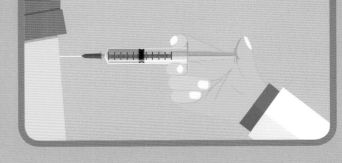

Public health

People are more likely to live longer and avoid disease if they are generally healthy. Access to clean water is key, as untreated water from lakes and rivers often contains bacteria that can cause serious disease. A balanced diet and the right amount of food are also important. Being hungry or malnourished makes people weaker and more likely to become ill.

This water pump in South Sudan has been built to give villagers access to clean, treated water that is safe to drink.

FOCUS ON Niger

Niger is a country in West Africa. It has the highest birth rate in the world and its population is growing quickly.

FACT FILE

- POPULATION GROWTH: **3.19%**
- AVERAGE CHILDREN BORN PER WOMAN: **6.49**
- AVERAGE AGE OF RESIDENT: **15.4 years**

Birth rate

There are several reasons for Niger's high birth rate. Agriculture is the country's main industry. Parents have large families so that their children can help on their farms. Women tend to get married and start having children early for religious and cultural reasons. This means that they are more likely to have bigger families.

This boy in Niger is helping with his family's herd of goats.

Land shortage

Around 80 per cent of people in Niger live in rural areas. Land is passed down through families and shared among children. Large family sizes mean that children are inheriting smaller pieces of land. It is hard for people to produce enough food to support themselves and make money from their small plots of land.

Almost 70% of Niger's population is under 25 years old.

The future

Most people in Niger are young. Soon, they will start to have their own children and the country's population will grow further. This will put even more pressure on resources in the country. To reduce the birth rate, Niger needs investment in new industries that can make the most of its large adult workforce. Improving the education of women and helping them to find jobs would also help.

FOCUS ON Russia

Russia is a large country in Europe and Asia. It has a negative population growth rate, which means that its population is decreasing every year. This is due to a combination of a low birth rate and a high death rate.

Birth rate

The low birth rate in Russia is partly due to poverty and low income. People don't want to risk having children that they might not be able to support. The Russian government is trying to encourage people to have more children by giving them money after the birth of their first child, but birth rates have not yet increased much.

A Russian grandmother looks after her grandson. Grandparents often help care for their grandchildren so that parents can work.

An ageing population

Russia's low birth rate means that its population is getting older. In the future, it will be a challenge for the limited population of young people to work to support the country's economy and take care of the large elderly population. Immigration and an increase in the birth rate would help to tackle this problem.

Marino Branch
Brainse Marino
Tel: 8336

Health issues

Life expectancy in Russia has been low since the 1990s. This is because of several issues, including poor nutrition, a lack of access to healthcare and high rates of smoking and alcohol use. Many areas also have high rates of air pollution, which can lead to disease.

Migration

Countries' populations are affected by migration. Immigration is when people come into a country to settle and emigration is when people leave a country.

Reasons for migration

People choose to settle in other countries for many reasons. Push factors are reasons why people leave a country. Pull factors are reasons why people choose to settle in a country.

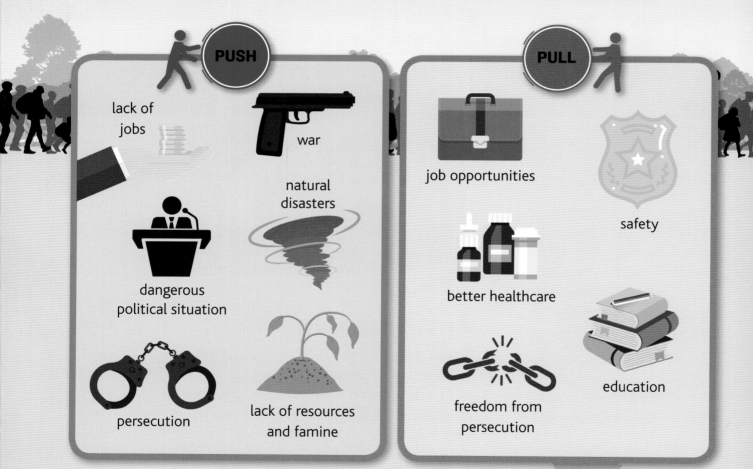

PUSH

lack of jobs

war

natural disasters

dangerous political situation

persecution

lack of resources and famine

PULL

job opportunities

safety

better healthcare

education

freedom from persecution

Overpopulated areas

Many people choose to leave overpopulated areas where there is competition for jobs, resources and housing. They move to areas with fewer people or more economic development.

War

Conflict can be more likely in overpopulated areas. When resources are stretched thin, arguments about land, food and water can quickly become violent. Experts believe that the rise of radical Islamist groups in the Middle East and north Africa may be linked to overpopulation in these areas (see pages 16–17).

By 2050, up to **200 million** people could have been forced to leave their homes because of global warming.

Climate change

Climate change is already starting to affect space and resources in some areas. Rising sea levels and flooding are making people flee their homes. Drought and extreme weather are damaging crops and causing food shortages. Countries near the equator in tropical areas will be the most affected by climate change. These countries are often less economically developed. Problems resulting from lack of space and resources in these areas will only get worse if climate change continues.

Benefits

There are many benefits to immigration. Countries with ageing populations and little population growth need young people to support the economy and take care of the elderly. Immigration also creates a richer, more diverse society.

Refugees from Syria and Afghanistan arrive in Germany. Germany has negative population growth, so immigrants will help to support the economy in years to come.

Drawbacks

Some people worry about the consequences of migration. An increase in population puts more pressure on a country's resources and space. However, this is only an issue in countries that are already suffering from overpopulation. Immigration benefits many countries, as immigrants contribute to the country's economy by working.

FOCUS ON Syria

Syria is in crisis. There has been a civil war in the country since 2011 and millions of Syrians have been forced to flee the country. In some part, this conflict can be linked to overpopulation, because of both population growth and a decrease in available resources.

FACT FILE

LOCATION:
Middle East

POPULATION:
18,028,000

NUMBER OF SYRIAN
REFUGEES: **4,000,000**

Rapid growth

In the second half of the twentieth century, Syria experienced rapid population growth. During this time, the country had a relatively successful economy. People were not encouraged to limit the number of children they had, so families became very large. The country was able to provide enough resources for its population and avoid overpopulation.

More resources

As time went on, more water and food was needed to support Syria's growing population. However, the country was unable to keep up with the demands of its population.

Syria's population grew from 3.25 million in 1950 to **22 million** in 2012.

Dreadful drought

Conditions were made worse by a terrible drought from 2006 to 2010. It was the worst drought experienced by Syria in 900 years. Scientists believe that this may have been a result of global warming. Crops failed year after year during the drought, affecting the country's economy and resulting in less food to go around.

On the move

As a result of the drought, around 1.5 million Syrians moved from the countryside to cities to find work. There was not enough housing to accommodate the new arrivals and many were forced to live in slum conditions. Education, healthcare and roads were put under pressure, and traffic, pollution and unemployment increased. Many new arrivals struggled to find jobs as they were not appropriately trained or educated. Food production decreased further as people left their farms behind.

Conflict

Tense conditions in Syrian cities played a key role in the uprising that eventually led to the start of the Syrian civil war in 2011. Since then, millions of Syrians have left the country to seek safety in neighbouring countries, such as Turkey, Lebanon, Jordan and Iraq. These countries are now dealing with their own overcrowding issues, as the sudden arrival of Syrian refugees has stretched their supply of resources.

Syrian refugees prepare to cross over the border into Turkey.

Resources

We all need natural resources to survive. The bigger the population on Earth, the more natural resources needed to keep everyone fed, housed and healthy. However, the Earth can only supply a limited amount of resources.

Resources to survive

People require a range of resources. We need food grown on fertile land or collected from the wild. We need materials such as wood, metal and stone, to construct buildings. Fuels are used in industry, and to power vehicles or produce electricity. We use water for drinking, cooking and cleaning (see pages 22–23).

Environmental damage

Our use of natural resources causes environmental damage. Cutting down trees for wood and to create farmland destroys natural habitats and can cause desertification, a process in which land eventually turns into desert. Burning fossil fuels (coal, oil and natural gas) contributes to the greenhouse effect, which leads to global warming and climate change.

Low supply

Our supply of fossil fuels is already running low. If we continue to use fossil fuels at current rates, the supply could be used up in the next 100 years. We can't run out of food, as we can always grow more crops or raise more livestock, as long as the climate remains stable. However, some countries are unable to produce enough food to support their population, due to weather conditions or lack of fertile land. Their citizens can't afford to buy imported food, so many go hungry.

A vicious cycle

The more resources we consume, the more we damage our planet, making it even harder to produce the resources that we need to survive. For example, burning fossil fuels leads to climate change. Climate change causes extreme weather. During periods of drought or heavy rainfall, many crops fail, affecting food supply.

Fewer resources

Less economically developed countries consume fewer resources per head. However, their high populations mean that this low consumption can add up overall. These countries also lack environmentally friendly technology, such as solar panels. They have to rely on polluting methods of generating power, such as burning wood.

This man in a rural part of India is gathering wood to burn as fuel.

More resources

Many citizens of more economically developed countries consume vast amounts of resources. They drive cars and live in large homes that require lots of energy to heat and cool. They buy huge quantities of products and food, which require resources for manufacturing and transportation. Even though more economically developed countries have lower populations, they still consume far more resources overall.

One small step

Around one third of all food produced globally goes to waste. Try not to buy excess food and use up all leftovers.

Solutions

More economically developed countries need to consume fewer resources and reduce waste. Less economically developed countries need to control population growth to reduce the amount of resources needed to support their population.

FOCUS ON

Drought-resistant crops

Rising temperatures and changes in rainfall caused by climate change threaten crops. Planting drought-resistant crops is one solution that could help to secure our food supply.

Drought has destroyed this field of corn.

Drought

In less economically developed countries, people get most of their calories from grains such as maize, wheat and rice. During periods of drought, these crops often fail. There is not enough fresh water to water crops. These countries often can't afford to invest in effective irrigation systems. This can lead to food shortages and famine, as farmers can't produce enough food to support the country's population.

Natural resistance

One solution is to stop growing maize, wheat, rice and other crops that are easily affected by drought, and to start planting naturally drought-resistant crops. These include grains such as sorghum, millet, pigeon peas and cowpeas.

Genetic modification

Scientists can also change the genetic structures of wheat, maize and rice to make them more resistant to drought. They can be modified (changed) to react more quickly to high temperatures or a lack of water, so that they don't lose as much water through evaporation.

Climate-change security

Planting drought-resistant crops will help to increase food security in the areas most affected by climate change. This is because farmers will still be able to grow the grains that people depend on as their main source of calories.

Over 5 years, yield across 13 African countries increased from 10% to 30% after changing to drought-resistant crops.

More food

At the moment, most grains do not produce a high yield — not all of the seeds planted produce crops that can be harvested. Grains can be genetically modified to produce a higher yield. This means that more farmers can produce more food to support people, even if the population grows.

Issues

Other countries need to support less economically developed countries during their transition to drought-resistant crops. Many farmers in less economically developed countries do not have the money to invest in new seeds. Some people don't trust the new seeds and are unwilling to plant them, as they are worried they will not grow properly. There are also fears about the long-term effects of using GM crops, as scientists have not yet been able to test them over a long period of time.

Water

Water is an incredibly important resource. However, if we don't keep our water supply clean and use it sustainably, we may run out of usable water to support our population.

Fresh water

Less than three per cent of the water on Earth is the fresh water that we need for drinking, cooking, watering plants, cleaning and most industry. The rest is salt water, found in seas and oceans. The amount of water on Earth will never increase or decrease. However, climate change is affecting the water cycle, leading to periods of drought, rising sea levels and heavy rain.

Pollution

Pollution from industry and poor sanitation affects our supply of clean, usable water. Water polluted with human waste and dangerous chemicals can make people ill and even kill them. Hundreds of millions of people around the world, mainly in less economically developed countries, do not have access to clean water.

2.3 billion people still do not have access to sanitary toilets.

India is making a huge effort to improve access to sanitary toilets. From 2014 to 2018, they increased the share of the population with household access from 42.8% to 88.9%.

Water consumption

Like all resources, water consumption is different in more and less economically developed countries. Most people in more economically developed countries have household appliances that consume large amounts of water, such as showers, dishwashers and washing machines. Even though less economically developed countries have larger populations, individual people usually use little water at home. Most water is used in industry and agriculture.

Cutting down

High consumption of water puts a strain on the already limited water supply. People should try to reduce their personal water consumption. We can also look at the amount of water used to grow or raise the food that we eat, and try to eat more foods that require less water.

One small step

Swap meat meals for vegetarian meals a few times a week.

It takes around **1,000 l of water** to produce a 150-g beef burger, but just **160 l** for a 150-g soy burger.

Saving water

To make water use more sustainable in less economically developed countries, it is important to invest in sanitation systems. More effective irrigation systems that use less water can be installed to help farmers reduce water use. Rainwater collection systems and reservoirs can be constructed to create back-up reserves of water for use during dry periods.

A sprinkler system irrigates this cabbage farm in Rajasthan, India.

Cities

As the world population grows, more space is needed for homes for everyone to live in. Cities with high-density housing are the most efficient way to fit a large number of people into one area.

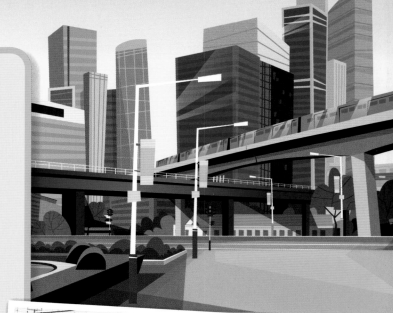

Country to city

Settlement patterns have changed over the past 200 years. In the past, there were a few cities, but most people lived in small villages and towns spread out over the countryside. Today, most people around the world live in cities.

Lagos, in Nigeria, is one of the fastest-growing cities in the world. Experts think that it may be the largest city in the world by 2100, with 85–100 million residents.

Moving to cities

People move to cities for many different reasons. Some move to find work. Many businesses and government organisations have offices in large cities, so there are more employment opportunities. Access to public services, such as healthcare and education, is also often better in cities, as there are more hospitals and schools.

Today, over **50%** of people live in cities.

Housing

Most cities have a high population density, with a large number of people living in a small area. There is not enough space to house everyone in large detached houses. Instead, many people live in smaller individual homes inside blocks of flats. Their outdoor space is made up of balconies, roof gardens and public parks.

Green cities

High-density city life can be environmentally friendly. Blocks of flats require less energy for heating. People can walk or cycle to offices, shops and services, which are usually close by. Public transport is easy to set up, as many people need to travel around the same area. However, if cities do not have the money to invest in public transport, car traffic can make cities polluted and unpleasant.

Different families

Population increase isn't the only reason why more houses are needed. In the past fifty years, changes in family set-ups mean that people need more individual homes than ever before. People are waiting longer to get married or staying single. More and more couples are getting separated or divorced. This is a bigger issue in more economically developed countries.

Mumbai

Mumbai is a city on the west coast of India. It is the most populated city in India and is one of the most densely populated cities in the world.

FACT FILE

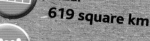

SIZE: 619 square km

POPULATION: 18,400,000

POPULATION DENSITY: 26,400 per square km

Moving to Mumbai

Mumbai has experienced dramatic population growth since the middle of the twentieth century, increasing from 1.6 million in 1941 to 18.4 million today. Immigration within India is the main reason for Mumbai's population increase. Many people move to the city looking for jobs, especially low-skilled workers who want to work in factories.

Overcrowding

The infrastructure in Mumbai has not kept up with its huge increase in population. Most people who earn average or low wages live in overcrowded, slum conditions. Public transport is severely overcrowded, which leads to dangerous stampedes on trains and at stations. As a result, many people drive instead, which clogs up roads with traffic jams.

A traffic jam brings cars, buses, rickshaws and motorbikes to a halt in Mumbai.

Slums

People living in slums experience poor living conditions and water supply. Most houses don't have attached bathrooms, so people have to leave their homes to use public bathrooms. Houses are small and cramped, with little ventilation.

Over **half** of Mumbai's population live in slums.

Investment

The Indian government is working to improve Mumbai, but some people believe that this investment does not benefit the majority of the people who live there. Slum housing in the city centre is being cleared for roads or new luxury buildings. The people who lived in the slums are being moved to poor-quality housing on the outskirts of the city, far from their jobs and families.

Air pollution

Mumbai is the fourth most polluted city in the world. Toxic fumes from vehicles and dust from new construction create air pollution. This can lead to breathing problems and lung diseases. As the city expands, new housing is being built on polluted former industrial areas. This air and ground pollution is affecting the health of the new residents.

Solutions

Everyone has a part to play in solving the issue of overpopulation. People in more economically developed countries need to focus on reducing the amount of natural resources they consume, while people in less economically developed countries need to work on maintaining the population at a reasonable size.

Resources

If people in more economically developed countries consumed fewer resources, there would be more to go around. By using less energy, and reusing and recycling items, we can easily reduce the amount of resources we use. It's also important not to waste food or water (see pages 19 and 23).

One small step

Repair or reuse old objects rather than buying new things. This uses fewer resources and helps to reduce waste.

Smaller families

In less economically developed countries, education and family planning programmes are the best way to keep family sizes under control. Educating women in rural areas and improving their access to healthcare helps to empower them and allows them to decide how many children they want to have.

Government control

In some countries, governments try to reduce the birth rate through taxes or fines. From 1979 to 2015, a Chinese policy forced parents to pay large amounts of money if they had more than one child. As a result, many families could only afford one child and the birth rate fell dramatically. By contrast, in some countries with low birth rates, such as South Korea and Russia (see page 13), governments are encouraging people to have children by offering them money after the baby's birth.

China's one-child policy prevented around **400 million** births.

A Chinese couple ride through the city of Xiang Yang with their daughter. Some Chinese couples still prefer to have one child for financial reasons.

Living space

As the world population grows, there may not be enough space for everyone in cities or other areas in which people prefer to live. The size of houses may need to get smaller. High-density housing options, such as flats, should be built as these are more space-efficient than large, detached houses.

Step by step

Overpopulation might seem like a huge problem that is impossible to solve. However, we can all take steps to help make a change. Read through this book for ideas. With an adult, research ways in which you can support people in other countries, such as sponsoring girls so that they can go to school.

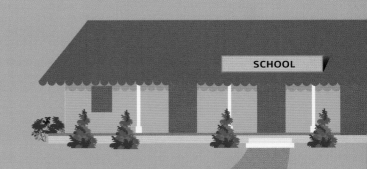

SCHOOL

Glossary

civil war a war fought between different groups of people living in the same country

crops plants that are grown in large amounts

density the number of people or objects compared to the size of an area

drought a period of time when there isn't enough water

family planning learning how to choose when to have children

famine a long period when people in an area do not have enough food, so they suffer and may die

fertile describes soil in which plants grow well

fossil fuel a fuel that comes from the ground, such as coal, oil or natural gas

greenhouse effect when certain gases gather in the Earth's atmosphere, trapping the Sun's heat close to the surface and making it warmer

income money earned from working

life expectancy the number of years that a person is expected to live

migration when people move to another country to live

poverty being very poor

resistant not harmed or affected by something

rural relating to the countryside

sanitation a system that protects people's health by removing waste

settlement a village, town or city

sustainable describes something that can continue for a long time because it does not harm the environment

tax money that you have to pay to the government from what you earn

tax haven a place where people don't have to pay very much tax

treated water water that has been processed so that it is safe to use

urban relating to cities

yield the amount of something that is produced

Further reading

EcoSteam: The Stuff We Buy by Georgia Amson-Bradshaw (Wayland, 2018)

Population and Settlement (Geographics) by Izzi Howell (Franklin Watts, 2017)

Population – Are There Too Many of Us? (Question it!) by Philip Steele (Wayland, 2017)

Websites

www.worldometers.info/world-population/
Keep up with the world population in real time.

www.bbc.co.uk/bitesize/ks3/geography/interdependence/population_migration/revision/3/
Read more about population density.

www.bbc.co.uk/newsround/33729890
Find out why some people are migrating to Europe.

easyscienceforkids.com/world-population-day-facts/
Learn some fun facts about population.

Note to parents and teachers:
Every effort has been made by the publisher to ensure that these websites contain no inappropriate or offensive material. However, because of the nature of the Internet, it is impossible to guarantee that the content of these sites will not be altered. We strongly advise that Internet access is supervised by a responsible adult.

Marino Branch
Brainse Marino
Tel: 8336297

Index

birth rates 4, 6, 9, 10, 11, 12, 13, 29

cities 7, 8, 17, 24–25, 26, 27, 29
climate change 5, 15, 18, 19, 20, 21, 22

drought 15, 17, 19, 20, 21, 22
drought-resistant crops 20–21

elderly, the 13, 15
emigration 14

family planning 10, 28
farming 9, 12, 17, 18, 20, 21, 23
food 4, 9, 10, 11, 12, 15, 16, 17, 18, 19, 20, 21, 23, 28

global warming 17, 18

healthcare 4, 13, 14, 17, 24, 28
housing 8, 14, 17, 19, 24, 25, 27, 29

immigration 9, 13, 14, 15, 26

medicine 11
migration 4, 9, 14–15
Mumbai 26–27

natural disasters 10, 14
Niger 12

pollution 5, 9, 13, 17, 19, 22, 25, 27
population density 6–7, 8, 25
population growth 4, 5, 11, 12, 13, 15, 16, 19, 25, 26
public transport 9, 25, 27

refugees 15, 17
Russia 13

sanitation 4, 5, 22, 23
Singapore 8–9,
slums 17, 27
Syria 15, 16–17

wars 10, 14, 15, 16, 17
water 4, 5, 9, 10, 11, 15, 16, 18, 20, 21, 22–23, 27, 28
world population 4, 5, 29

ECOGRAPHICS

Series contents lists

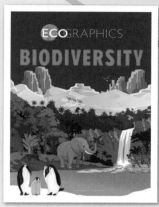

BIODIVERSITY

HB: 978 1 4451 6596 7
PB: 978 1 4451 6597 4

● What is biodiversity? ● Genetic diversity ● Ecosystems ● Focus on keystone species ● Deforestation ● Focus on the Amazon Rainforest ● Climate change ● Pollution ● Hunting ● Focus on the ivory trade ● Invasive species ● Consequences ● Back from the brink ● Focus on the bald eagle ● Focus on the humpback whale

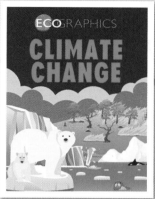

CLIMATE CHANGE

HB: 978 1 4451 6571 4
PB: 978 1 4451 6572 1

● What is climate change? ● Fossil fuels ● Global warming ● Rising sea levels ● Focus on the Greenland ice sheet ● Farming and food ● Habitats and wildlife ● Focus on sea turtles ● Desertification ● Focus on desertification in China ● Extreme weather ● Focus on Hurricane Harvey ● Stopping climate change

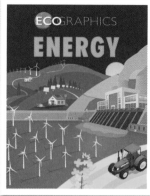

ENERGY

HB: 978 1 4451 6644 5
PB: 978 1 4451 6645 2

● What is energy? ● Fossil fuels ● Focus on natural gas ● Nuclear power ● Solar power ● Focus on California ● Hydroelectric power ● Focus on the Itaipu Dam ● Biomass ● Wind power ● Geothermal energy ● Focus on Iceland ● The future of energy

NATURAL RESOURCES

HB: 978 1 4451 6598 1
PB: 978 1 4451 6599 8

● What are natural resources? ● Resource distribution ● Oil, gas and coal ● Focus on Arctic oil ● Wood ● Focus on reforestation ● Metal and stone ● Focus on rare earth metals ● Water ● Farming ● Wildlife ● Focus on bees ● Recycling ● Managing natural resources

OVER POPULATION

HB: 978 1 4451 6642 1
PB: 978 1 4451 6643 8

● What is overpopulation? ● Distribution and density ● Focus on Singapore ● Births and deaths ● Focus on Niger and Russia ● Migration ● Focus on Syria ● Resources ● Focus on drought-resistant crops ● Water ● Cities ● Focus on Mumbai ● Solutions

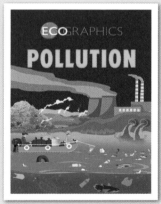

POLLUTION

HB: 978 1 4451 6600 1
PB: 978 1 4451 6601 8

● What is pollution? ● Water ● Focus on Lake Erie ● Ocean plastic ● Focus on the Great Pacific Garbage Patch ● Landfills ● Air ● The greenhouse effect ● Focus on air pollution in India ● Nuclear waste ● Focus on Fukushima ● Light and sound ● Reducing pollution

FRANKLIN WATTS